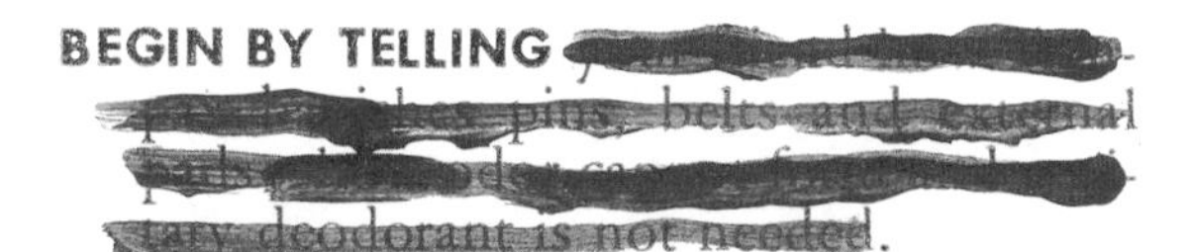

BEGIN BY TELLING [illegible]
[illegible] pins, belts and external
[illegible]
tary deodorant is not needed.

ALSO EXPLAIN [illegible] T[illegible]
no bulges or ridges under any costume
[illegible] how it is really [illegible] use and
can even be worn in a tub of [illegible]er.

THEN SHOW HER WHY [illegible]
about all these improve[illegible]
vention by a doctor, its *internal absorp-*
tion [illegible]
tion, its tremendous absorbency, its
patented [illegible] that makes inser-
tion so quick and easy.

SEND HER OUT TO BUY [illegible]
drug sto[illegible]
[illegible] zes [illegible]
Super and Junior. [illegible]
supply will slip into her pu[illegible]
Economy box contains 4 months' average [illegible] rpor-
ated, Pal[illegible]s.

BEGIN BY TELLING

Meg Remy

Illustrated by Logan T. Sibrel

BOOK*HUG PRESS 2021
ESSAIS SERIES NO. 11

FIRST EDITION

LIBRARY AND ARCHIVES CANADA CATALOGUING IN PUBLICATION

Title: Begin by telling / Meg Remy ; illustrated by Logan T. Sibrel.
Names: Remy, Meg, 1985- author. | Sibrel, Logan T., illustrator.
Series: Essais (Toronto, Ont.) ; no. 11.
Description: First edition. | Series statement: Essais series ; no. 11 | Includes bibliographical references.
Identifiers: Canadiana (print) 2021010418X | Canadiana (ebook) 20210104384
ISBN 9781771666633 (softcover) | ISBN 9781771666640 (EPUB)
ISBN 9781771666657 (PDF) | ISBN 9781771666664 (Kindle)
Subjects: LCSH: Remy, Meg, 1985- | LCSH: Musicians—United States—Biography. | LCSH: Women musicians—United States—Biography. | LCGFT: Autobiographies.
Classification: LCC ML420.R346 A3 2021 | DDC 782.42164092—dc23

PRINTED IN CANADA

The production of this book was made possible through the generous assistance of the Canada Council for the Arts and the Ontario Arts Council. Book*hug Press also acknowledges the support of the Government of Canada through the Canada Book Fund and the Government of Ontario through the Ontario Book Publishing Tax Credit and the Ontario Book Fund.

Canada Council for the Arts Conseil des Arts du Canada

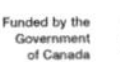

Book*hug Press acknowledges that the land on which we operate is the traditional territory of many nations, including the Mississaugas of the Credit, the Anishnabeg, the Chippewa, the Haudenosaunee, and the Wendat peoples. We recognize the enduring presence of many diverse First Nations, Inuit, and Métis peoples and are grateful for the opportunity to meet and work on this territory.

I tell what I have seen and what I believe;
and whoever shall say that I have not seen what I have seen,
I now tear off his head.
–Antonin Artaud

An abnormal reaction to an abnormal situation
is normal behavior.
–Viktor Frankl

Sesame Street is on top of me. It's resting against my face. What I thought was squishable proves to be flat and staticky when touched. I'm an age that feels too fresh for a memory—someone still changes my diapers—but the TV has fallen on me. The impact is profound. Though I suffer no physical injury, I can never forget what I saw. The TV screen is made up of tiny shapes and lines working in tandem to create The Big Picture, like staring at the dog in the yard through the screen door.

I don't know if Babysitter Mom told Birth Mom the TV fell on me (it's not really important, seeing as I barely bother to differentiate; together they form a resounding singular MOM). It helps me to believe I got myself out from under the TV.

The funny figures I see on the screen I see on the floor because I'm falling asleep on top of a Sesame Street sheet at Grandma and Grandpa's. Music that sounds wobbly (crooners, I now know) is playing low on the bedside radio. Grandma's solution when you miss Mom is to put her framed high school portrait and a flashlight down next to you (the sweetness of this gesture still nourishing). I can understand Grandma is Mom's mom.

I watch people party in a strange way on top of a graffiti-slathered wall. The Wall looks larger than life-size on our big screen. Men who've been drinking lots of beer are hitting, kind of dancing, on The Wall with hammers and fists and feet. Dad on this side of the screen is acting proud and responsible: *Imagine if you went to the store and there was only one type of bread you could buy or one type of shoe. Choices!*

"Wind of Change" by Scorpions is the audio that gets fused to this memory. Maybe "Wind of Choice" would have been a better title? Both titles make me think Farts. What is Berlin?

On the same big screen, we watch Pink Floyd's *The Wall*. Is this the same The Wall?

When a brick of The Wall, not sure which The Wall, shows up at our house, out of place as a moon rock, I'm stuck somewhere just beyond my grasp of history and memorabilia.

Our chunk of The Wall gets used as a paperweight.

Brother is in the hospital, gone totally pale grey but red around the eyes. There is a small TV floating heavy in the corner of the windowless (was it windowless?) room. It is showing the grand finale of what is clearly the most important fireworks display of all time, Dessert Storm! I see piles of candy and sundaes laced with razor blades, thunderheads of whipped cream, and a general with so many toys that his name is General FAO Schwarz.

No, no, no. It's Desert Storm, one s.
OR
Choices! Operation Desert Shield, the Gulf War, Persian Gulf War, the First Gulf War, Gulf War I, First Iraq War, Kuwait War.
OR
A triple series of **Topps** playing cards, exactly like the sports cards boys have binders full of.

Series 1 – Coalition for Peace
Series 2 – Victory Series
Series 3 – Homecoming Edition

Finally, memorabilia I can understand. I shuffle through them like they're part of some memory matching game. **Daddy's Home, Carpet Bombing, Stopping the Oil's Flow...**

The newspaper issued a large map complete with flags...and the instruction to *Flag the Movement of the Allied Forces from Day to Day*, as if the affair were a game.
–Janet Frame

Vacation in Myrtle Beach, South Carolina, with the same family we always take these kinds of trips with, because the children line up in age and we get along. The daughter-in-my-age-slot and me play mini-golf, feet away from our family suites. My turn to putt again. I decide to wind up like a pro and really whack the ball. It flies over or through a row of hedges into what we know on the other side is The Main Drag. No big thing. We have retrieved balls, kicked balls, racked balls, caught balls, dodged balls, served balls, teed up balls, inflated balls our whole life. We are old enough to do this.

We cross to the other side of the hedge and I spot the one that got away. (I believe I look both ways.) I start out across the multilane blacktop but don't get far. Something flashes out of the corner of left eye. Body puts hands up just in time for the loudest sound I've ever felt. I'm fly---ing through the air, suddenly silent and magical. Now I'm skid-d-d-ing, exposed flesh kissing and rubbing asphalt as sound returns.

People I don't know gather above me. *I'm-a-nurse* takes off her shirt to reveal a sports bra. *Don't move an inch...hit by a van.* Someone is screaming. It's just my friend, she's fine, always trying to make it about her. The sun is beating down on the scene. Cold sweat mixing with my blood, now peppered with little street rocks. I can feel when Mom is notified. I can hear her fear-footsteps landing one after the other, getting closer to what her new reality could be. When the paramedics arrive, I accept this fate. I am put on a stiff board with a neck brace and I am taken to a hospital in my bathing suit.

Mom and I take a cab back from the hospital to the hotel. I get out sore, shoeless, and road-rashed, but really actually fine, physically. People on a balcony somewhere are applauding the miracle. I know that if people are applauding me, Dad will be calling. I don't feel like explaining. I want to disappear into something larger than anything having to do with me. I will never hear the end of this. They'll all say I got hit chasing a ball like a dog. Your story in the wrong hands can be such a cruel poker.

The something larger arrives the next morning in the form of a rental truck full of explosives in Oklahoma City.* I watch the aftermath on a wood-paneled hotel TV that sits on top of a bureau in front of the bed I'm recovering in. I don't cry at the images or testimonies. Newly scabbed Body feels acknowledged by the screen. Was my accident some kind of foreshadowing? If only I could have warned all those babies! Yes, this is somehow My Fault. But why were there so many babies in a government building to begin with?** I see babies running the show: babies with gavels in their hands, babies with guns, babies as lawyers, incarcerated babies, little baby Betsy Ross with an American flag diaper.

*Timothy McVeigh, someone's son who built the bomb and lit the fuses, was a decorated veteran of ~~Dessert~~ Desert Storm. His last meal was two pints of mint chocolate chip ice cream.

**Because of a day-care center on the first floor. The image of an Oklahoma City firefighter cradling a bloody chalky dead baby in little white socks became the global representative of the event. Aren Almon, the mother of Baylee, the baby in the white socks: *Every time I went to the store, it was on the front of magazines. I would go to the doctor's office and there it was. On every television show, every news station, on the front of T-shirts, on coffee mugs. It was everywhere and it was devastating. It broke my heart that she had to be seen that way. I have no rights to that picture at all. I can't say how it's used.*

The photographer was awarded a Pulitzer for the photo. Cruel pokers everywhere.

I want to die because I can't be alive in the 1960s. Each episode of the *Beatles Anthology* TV series rips a strip off me. I dream of John Lennon eight days a week. I'm disappointed Mom didn't drop out of high school and move to San Francisco. *If I had been alive back then...*

She takes you to see "The Beatles" at the Rialto Theater. You scream like bloody-Beatlemania-murder! After the show you take your beloved *Anthology* Christmas present book to the autograph area. "John," "Paul," "George," and "Ringo" sign the book, just like that, with quotes, maybe so they don't get sued. "Ringo" puts a peace sign outside his quotes.

American English in concert perform songs covering the entire career of The Beatles from 1963-1970. With precise attention to every musical detail, along with costume changes, vintage instruments, and special effects, American English magically create a tribute to The Beatles you won't soon forget.
–americanenglish.com

I remember looking down at the cinema floor and seeing these rivulets of piss in the aisles. The girls were literally pissing themselves with excitement. So what I associate most with The Beatles is the smell of girls' urine.
–Bob Geldof

It wasn’t pee in my underwear. It was blood.

You're a woman!
I'm holding bloody undies for inspection between thumb and pointer finger as Mom hugs me. She makes a real day out of it. We picnic in a park a few towns over. I'm allowed to ask her anything and she tells me what she thinks I need to know (*It's a different hole from where pee comes out...*). But I already know too much and I don't have the heart to burst her bubble. The sun is witnessing us. I feel part of something ancient and precarious.

Mom's best friend sends me a card in the mail:
WELCOME TO THE CLUB!
The rules of The Club are ambiguous. I don't wanna do anything to get kicked out. I dream of being an astronaut but how can I be an astronaut with a period? Zero gravity blood flowing and floating all over the capsule, jamming up the electronics, NASA regretting the day they ever let women go up there. Please don't let me be the woman who ruins the space program.

I am disturbed by psychic ignition. Stomach ejects itself out of burning Body, out into some non-Earth dimension of nausea. A zebra stripe runs through the middle of my vision and shakes everything I see. I go to Mom. *Something bad is going to happen.* She wants to know what. I can't tell her what, I just Know. This is not the first/last time I will Know something, so she knows to believe me.

In fact, Mr. Bin Laden takes them [dreams] so seriously that he says he was afraid that the visionaries and dreamers would give the World Trade Center plot away: 'I was worried that maybe the secret would be revealed if everyone starts seeing it in their dream.' So he tells a dreaming man in Kandahar 'not to tell anybody' his dreams about an airplane.
–Sarah Boxer

The next morning I'm suffering a brutal hyper-vigilance hangover after tossing and turning all night on patrol along the zebra line. I go back to sleep in Mom's bed. She leaves the TV on for me, calls school to tell them I won't be there, and goes off to work.

Ears wake up. The voices on the TV have that special breaking-news sound that makes the hairs pulse till standing on end before turning to water. Something is unfolding the wrong way. The rest of Body starts to move and reach for glasses, puts them on to look at Mom's trusty TV. I see the building swallow the violence whole like it's familiar with that exact dose. The zebra stripe disappears.

How many people were raped at the World Trade Center?

Unfortunately, there is a lack of dialogue between those who study daily secrets and those who study state secrets.
–Eviatar Zerubavel

I watch weeks of TV, trying to answer this seemingly unconnected question that appears out of nowhere and refuses to leave me alone. All I Know is I don't trust The World Trade Center. Something just ain't right about that place.

Never Forget

to connect the dots.

This book is an attempt to connect a couple.

Fifteen years later Kassie and I are driving all around New York's Financial District. *It's supposed to be here! Let's park and walk around. Might be easier to find on foot.* We finally find what we are looking for outside of a Verizon Wireless store. It's coated in plastic to protect it from the weather. It's about the size of a poster board.

How come The World Trade Center gets a big billion-dollar memorial and New York's Municipal Slave Market–prong genesis of America (no World Trade Center without it)–gets a plastic sign that must compete for space with a no-dog-poop signpost? Don't say there is already a slavery memorial in NYC. These are not arbitrary choices. There is no random when it comes to violence or memorials.

Abridged List of Violence You Witnessed Between 2004 and 2012

–The man who pulls a knife at the record store. Everyone runs while you stay. Nothing comes of it.

–Two men behind Home Depot in some road-rage affair bashing each other's brains in. No one sees but you. The two cars come to a screech right where you are walking. Lovers finally behind closed doors, they rush toward each other for a red-faced embrace. Words barely form on their lips as spit and fists fly. You find it horrific, then boring. You walk away.

–Pregnant woman shot multiple times in front of your apartment. She and the never-to-be-born baby lie dead inside a pink tracksuit, visible from your front window. The cops seem more interested in whether or not you and your roommate have boyfriends. You are the only ones on the block who talk to the cops. You now recognize a difference between you and your neighbors: you have experienced no (conscious) reason to fear the cops and your neighbors have experienced all the reasons to fear the cops.

–The man at Kinko's who pulls a gun over $4 in faxes (not sure if he didn't have the money to pay or was offended to be charged in the first place). The impressively calm employee who has the gun pointed in her face doesn't see the point in calling the cops.

You agree, stay, and finish your copies.

–You're sitting on a subway train. A man who smells something on you comes right over to tell you about it (*fucking American!*) by spit-spit-spitting on you. You stand up for leverage, having always known you don't wanna get stabbed from above. Eye to eye would be best. You stand your ground only because you are frozen in place, in fear. No one helps you, though everyone watches. When the train reaches the next stop, you flee, you don't know where you are, you see cops and you yell and point at the man who spit on you. They get on the train with him, the doors close, and the train pulls away. You are hyperventilating. You turned someone in even though you Know better.

–We are finally Single and in the same city. The consensual dance we had choreographed over all those years will finally get its performance. We get drunk but he's able to drive us to his pull-up-to-the-door motel. The door closes past me, sucking all the oxygen out with it. Quickly he forms and holds tight a strange cross, his forearm against my throat, while spitting on my face between grunts of choking phrases. *Don't gotta tell me twice! I'm outta here!* I abandon Body and witness from a safe distance up in the right-hand corner of the room, turning my gaze between the scene of *The Cosby Show* on mute (did he turn the TV on?) and the scene of us on the bed. I come down from the corner just in time to watch his naked behind walk into the bathroom. I think I laugh out loud.

If I was insane, everything could be made to make sense. If I was sane, nothing could.
–Tara Westover

(I took accountability/ownership for this event so that someone would, because I knew you wouldn't, or maybe I didn't have the energy to see if you would. I was exhausted from being choked and spit on. You could have asked to choke me and spit in my face. Maybe I would have said yes? I wanted the sex part.)

THE
COSBY
SHOW

It was your typical yellow school bus in all the familiar ways except the SHOW US YOUR TITS written in white shoe polish on the windows. I guess if they had written PLEASE MAY WE SEE YOUR BREASTS it would not have had the same effect.

Demand vs. Request.

Wait...maybe it said SHOW US YOUR HOOTERS. I can't be sure. I don't have a photo of the bus. Body just has a feeling.

We do not see anything in the eye.
–M. Luckiesh

Show Us
YOUR tits

show us yoUR
HOOtERS

This yellow bus is a family business vehicle, and inside are male kin on their way to the Indianapolis 500.* *The Greatest Spectacle in Racing* is when 300,000+ spectators bake in the mad Memorial Day sun as thirty-three single-seater open-cockpit race cars throb around a rectangle with rounded corners for 200 laps. That's 500 miles of BYOB, it being the single largest sporting event that allows folks to bring in their own coolers (oh, strange the times Capitalism strategically chooses to pause!). From a different type of cooler, the winner of the race is given milk, his choice between whole, 2%, and skim. He must drink the Official Milk or be excommunicated (dairy lobbyists are powerful). I say "his"/"he" because a woman has never won the Indianapolis 500 and I bring up this "woman stuff" only because I'm still trying to figure out why they wrote SHOW US YOUR TITS on that bus. Is it because milk comes from tits?

The penis or Phallus would take the place of the breast as invested object of interest. The boy's mark 'gives' him privilege, because it puts him in the 'superior' category–in a manipulative, if 'x' then 'y' way–while the mother's breasts gave to him directly. Its erotization coincides with the estrangement of the boy into the privileged, non-nurturing category.
–Genevieve Vaughan

No one got curious about what was here before.
–Lee Maracle

*Slang: Indy. I'm sorry to say that not until I was in my twenties did I sort out that Indiana, where I spent every mandatory holiday, means Indian Land. It's interesting how many US state names tell on themselves. The truth rolling off our tongues.

Thoughts While Watching Game 7 of the 2019 World Series

Are those the richest people in Texas? The ones sitting behind home plate for Game 7, their personal waiters distracting. It's odd to watch someone order hot dogs and beer behind a batter, a catcher, an ump, a net, through a TV. Am I witnessing disagreeing familiars switching seats? The richest people in Texas must have two seats behind home plate for Game 7 AND a skybox. (A skybox is like an opera box on a Transformer, a place to watch war comfortably. It's where Ellen DeGeneres sat next to George Bush.) They are forced to take turns two at a time, down in the dirt, to ensure an authentic baseball experience for the whole family. Otherwise it would be only real towels in the bathroom, dessert cart after the seventh-inning stretch, too air-conditioned to be legit. Two lively women have settled into those seats behind home plate. Women love sports but sports do not love women back. They stand up for a selfie when the batter bats and the men around them go red mad. I think I hear the B word through the screen. Never call a mom a B! How to total up the free labor that goes into making a pro athlete? What would the dollar figure be on moms cleaning those endless loads of putrid high school practice clothes? Not to mention the actual delivery of the pro! Imagine the value of the time fans spend being fans. Free brand ambassadors.

No, paying the brand to be its brand ambassador. This is what we do. Osuna on the mound. I'm trying to feel empathy.*

The policy seems to have caused some teams, like the Yankees and Astros, to view players suspended for domestic abuse as some sort of inefficiency, using the suspension as leverage to acquire those players at a lower cost.
–Sheryl Ring, Esq.

*Roberto Osuna was the eighth MLB player to be disciplined under the new (as of 2016) MLB domestic violence policy. The MLB and its policy are incapable of addressing an issue as complex as domestic abuse while concurrently acquiring and selling humans in an attempt to win/make a profit.

She'll take a few balls under the chin
to get ahold of your high hard one.

Does anyone remember Big Johnson? I ask a candlelit dinner party. No one seems to understand what I am asking. The next time I ask I ask Kassie. She remembers Big Johnson T-shirts walking down the halls of her high school. Since then I found out the guy has a real name:

E. Normus Johnson

I don't know who the wearers of these shirts were in my life. They just seem to have always been there. There was a camping-themed one I would stare into as if it were a Magic Eye with a message for me:

Big Johnson Pup Tents: When you're going deep in the bush, it pays to have a Big Johnson

The silk-screenie illustration: E. Normus lying on his back in a tent, his Big Johnson obviously "the tent pole," a large-breasted severely cross-eyed blonde looking on.

What would be the daily reality of a person with a five-foot penis? (This talk of length makes me feel insecure about the length of this text. Will it be long enough to be deemed Book?*)

Here quantification begins to be important, because the quantity (size) of the phallus may appear to be the reason the father, not the boy, is in the polarized 'one' position. Phallic quantity seems to be the most important quality. –Genevieve Vaughan

*The publisher answers this question when I submit my first draft, saying the only issue that needs to be addressed is the length. They didn't get my joke.

INT. - COCKPIT OF EA-18G GROWLER JET

Two junior officers from the Electronic Attack Squadron 103 conduct a routine training exercise in a clear blue sky over North Central Washington State.

Bored with their exercise, the officers get creative.

EWO (Electronic War Officer)
Draw a giant penis. That would be awesome.

PILOT
(joking) What did you do on your flight? Oh, we turned dinosaurs into sky penises.

EWO
You should totally try to draw a penis.

PILOT
(Boastful tone) I could definitely draw one, that would be easy. I could basically draw a figure eight and turn around and come back.

(Maneuvering jet to begin marking the sky)

I'm gonna go down, grab some speed, and hopefully get out of the contrail layer so they're not connected to each other.

EWO

Dude, that would be so funny. Airliner's coming back on its way into Seattle just this big fucking giant penis.

(The jet begins marking the sky)

EWO

We could almost draw a vein in the middle of it too.

PILOT

Balls are going to be a little lopsided...

(Jet arching)

Balls are complete. I just gotta navigate a bit over here for the shaft.

EWO

Which way is the shaft going?

PILOT

The shaft will go to the left

(Jet banks hard to the left)

EWO

It's gonna be a wide shaft…

PILOT

I don't wanna make it just like three balls…

EWO

Let's do it. Oh, the head of that penis is going to be thick.

PILOT

To get out of this, I'm gonna go like down and to the right and we'll come back up over the top and try to take a look at it. (disappointed tone) I have a feeling the balls will have dissipated by then.

The Growler flies away from the giant sky penis in order to view it at a distance. Laughing, the officers take photos of their artwork.

Low fuel warning begins to sound(BEEP! BEEP! BEEP!). The Growler swiftly returns to Naval Air Station Whidbey Island.

The average jet fuel consumption rate (based on typical operations patterns) of an EA-18G Growler is 1,304 gallons per hour[...] One hour of a single EA-18G Growler flight is equivalent to driving a typical car 29,500 miles. A single EA-18G Growler flying overhead makes as much CO_2 as 656 average US cars driving...
–Chris Greacen, PhD

Someone spilled crude oil in the Buick. I was blamed but I didn't do it. I remember seeing the jars on the floor, mason jars of crude oil at various stages of refinement, visual aids for Dad's patent pitches.

The smell lingered in the Buick. Stomach would turn each time I sat down in its beige Buick interior. Not because the smell was awful-sweaty-hairspray-tang, but because I Knew I was in for The Long Haul. The Buick had to be replaced because of the smell (or because of the divorce?). They say there is sweet crude oil and sour crude oil, depending on the level of sulfur in the stuff. Sweet crude oil is what they make gasoline out of, and that makes sense of why sometimes gas smells addictive, but it must have been the sour stuff that spilled in the Buick.

I play Elly Mae, Jed Clampett's tomboy daughter, in a skit for the school talent show.

Come and listen to my story about a man
named Jed,
A poor mountaineer, barely kept his family fed,
And then one day he was shootin at some food,
And up through the ground come a bubblin
crude.
Oil that is, black gold, Texas tea.

–*Beverly Hillbillies* theme song, 'The Ballad of Jed Clampett'

It wasn't Dad's connection to oil, but rather my tits (big for my age, big for my school) and blond hair–attributes of Elly Mae–that gave me the idea to do the skit in the first place. But it's true I was the only one who understood what "Texas tea" meant.

I pretend to be the daughter of a hypothetical man, a union man, as part of a mock trial for the entertainment of employees of Dad. In dirty jeans and flannel, with a busted-up cap on my head and soot from a fireplace on my face, I "testify" about the conditions of a union household in front of the laughing non-union petrochemical crowd.

I can't remember a line of the script that was coached into me but I know there was a bit of improv. He left it open so I could insert myself into the character. Game recognizes game. Play on, player.

Something compelled me to put the idea to tape. I guess Body was behind the wheel. I used the boom box with the built in-mic. I practiced each character's voice a few times, then I laid it down, a sexy radio play between Bill, Monica,* Hillary, and Chelsea. Classic porn scenario where Bill and Monica are getting busy, then Hillary walks in! She is initially angry but is persuaded to drop her beef and join them in ecstasy. Daughters don't like to be left out, so at the very end, Chelsea is permitted entry, making it an orgy.

Q: What about the radio address, Mr. President?

PRESIDENT CLINTON: Let me back up a second... I knew about the radio address. I was sick after it was over...

I did maybe two takes, then I masturbated along to the tape.

*Monica Lewinsky's internship was unpaid.

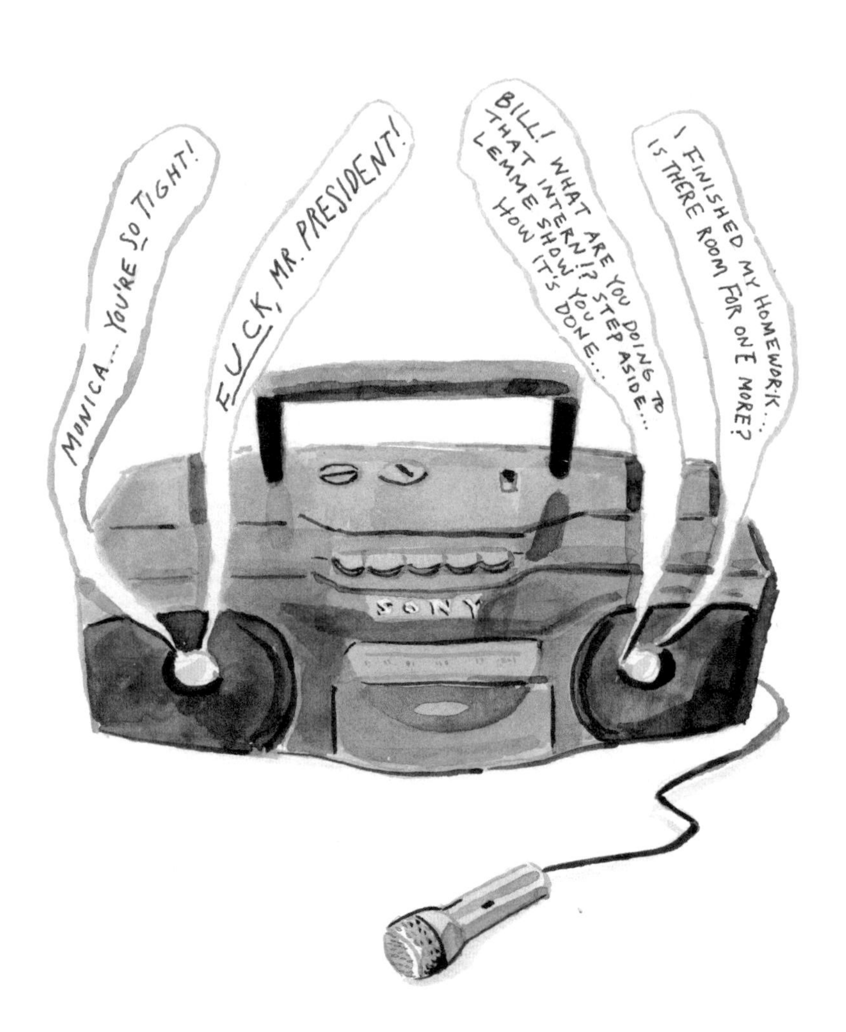
MONICA... YOU'RE SO TIGHT!
FUCK, MR. PRESIDENT!
BILL! WHAT ARE YOU DOING TO THAT INTERN!? STEP ASIDE... LEMME SHOW YOU HOW IT'S DONE...
I FINISHED MY HOMEWORK... IS THERE ROOM FOR ONE MORE?
SONY

I Knew the evidence (blue Gap dress) had to be destroyed so I dissolved the tape in some way now lost to time and
I didn't tell anyone
I had been raped.

That's not entirely accurate. I had told Sarah, but that was well before the sex tape. We were miles away from home, sitting on a dock by a lake. I can't remember the words I used or how she responded or what we did after. Of course, I swore her to secrecy and no doubt she swore she was a vault, but you can't hold another's secret for long. It's like the hottest potato.

[King Midas's barber] swore a solemn oath never to tell, but the secret so weighed upon the man that he finally went and dug a hole in a field and spoke into it, 'King Midas has asses' ears.' Then he felt relieved and filled the hole up. But in the spring reeds grew up there, and when stirred by the wind they whispered those buried words...
–Edith Hamilton

Sarah dropped my potato (I should have told the girl at school with the dripping chocolate strawberry-with-a-bite-out-of-it tattoo)! A complaint was filed via the Department of Children & Family Services. I was not prepared for what would be required to prove my experience. I spotted this right away and bailed.

My response to the allegations:

I never said that.

Response some people heard:

I lied.

I was stoned to near death by the word *recant* and I didn't even know what it meant. It became such a debate that money was in the future of those who would sign a sheet of paper stating they heard me say *I lied*. And I had lied, just not how they thought I did.

I lied to conceal having told the truth.

I can see now that everything I (we) did (do), everything I (we) said (say) was (is) a spilling of the beans, a constant begging to either be helped or put out of my (our) misery. The powers that be felt they had no choice left and the door was removed from the hinges of my teenage bedroom. Oh, to be punished for finding and using unconventional ways to survive! Cutting on my arms and stomach with an X-Acto made perfect sense to me and I still stand by it as what I needed to do at that time, but I wonder, where does the cutter's idea come from?

Architects add to the load when trying to strengthen a decrepit arch.
–Viktor Frankl

It has never been shown that punishment works. Punishment, denouncing, excluding, threatening, and shunning often create a worse society. It divides people...obscures truths in the name of falsely shoring up group reputation... [T]here is no correlation between having the ability to punish and being right.
–Sarah Schulman

For years of my adult life I said,

When I used to have sex with...
instead of
When I was raped by...

How smart of me to be euphemistic! (Sex is much lighter to carry than rape.) I had unconsciously fashioned myself into a magnet for risk, pain, guilt, and embarrassment. The closer my environment/chemicals mimicked the states of abuse I had experienced, the more secure I felt, the more sane. This is called coping.

A sordid encounter can blunt the abused child's horror and shame, if only for a couple hours.
–Bessel van der Kolk, MD

There isn't much to do at a wrestling tournament if you are just the younger sister of a wrestler. You find another sister who has a wrestling brother. Together you walk endless loops around the gymnasium, desperate for boys not busy on the mats.

You find two boys whose team was knocked out in the first round. The four of you find a smaller gymnasium that is unlocked, storage of mats its only purpose for the day.

We listen to alternative music through a Walkman with the headphones turned up and out. We tumble on the mats and it soon evolves into a different type of fooling around. We lie close to each other, eventually across each other, I observe the boys' cauliflower ears.* We smoke weed out of a corroded, stinking pipe. The lighter used to ignite the seedy weed somehow finds its way into my jeans, under underwear, into vagina. The boys are conducting some sort of science experiment on me. I like the one with greasy, longish hair more than the other one, but I let them both. My friend feels left out and leaves. I worry she is going to tell on me so I get my clothes sorted and follow her.

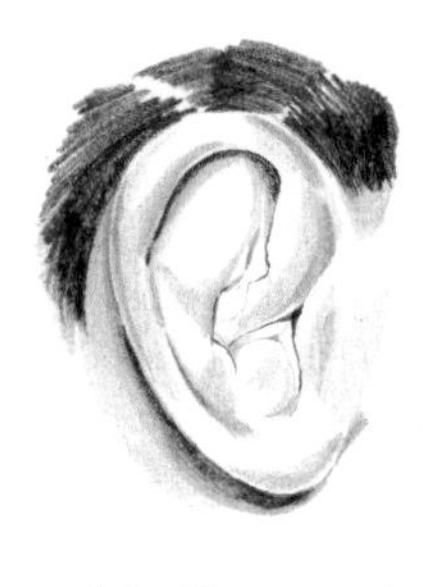

*Cauliflower ear is a condition that occurs in ears that are repeatedly slammed or hit. The delicate whirls and curls of the ear get filled, the details swollen away. It is common in wrestlers, rugby players, MMA fighters. It's an irreversible sculpture; the ears just stay that way. I spot these ears out in the wild a few times a year. *Hey, were you a wrestler?*

We return to our seats before victory hits. No one noticed we were ever gone. We catch the countdown and the celebration. I'm pumped on secrecy. Vagina is annoyed with me. Winning tears are all around. I see the boy I preferred exiting the gym, taking my consciousness with him. I will think of nothing but him for the next few days of my eleven-year-old life.

Back home, another State Championship secured, in a moment of obsessive brilliance, I remember THE PROGRAM. The commemorative program for the tournament has a photo and breakdown of every team. I run to it panting. I quickly find My Boy. I know his last name now.

The next time I am alone in the house, I grab the phone and dial 411. I give the operator My Boy's town, last name, and first name (in case he's a Jr.). In return I am given multiple possible matches. I take them all. I breathe deep and play the lottery. I land on the winning number! The boy comes to the phone and is shocked it's me. He couldn't be more disgusted. The call ends awkwardly. Body desires a setting different than the living room with Mom's cherrywood divorce furniture. Body wants to be in an alleyway facedown or in a pasture, under hoof.

I fell instantly in love with a ginger Dead Head. I passed by him riding in the back of a golf cart with the same girl who saw me get hit by the van. He had long enough hair for me to be impressed. We didn't speak, but possibility still passed between us. He was with another boy...man? This boy-man I already knew. He lived down the road. All our brothers were friends. My girlfriend had kissed this boy-man once or twice so she was allowed to say Hello. I didn't say a word. As soon as the guys were two tie-dyed dots in the distance, I demanded the scoop. She said she could get the ginger's number from the caller ID at her house. She promised she would.

She came through with the digits. I was bold enough to call him and he was always stoned enough to answer and chat. Often someone else was on the line, someone older and aggressive. I Knew I had gotten into something I'd be lucky to get out of alive.

They found out where I lived because maybe I told them. They would call to give me the *We're on our way*. I'd pace the twentyish minutes I knew the drive took. Then (if I could) I'd light a smoke and post up in the driveway. They'd cruise by slowly and I'd pose for them sometimes with a prop like the big rock at the end of the driveway.

One day they finally stopped. I went to the passenger window. The ginger was hiding in the back seat.

Boy-men in front were snarling, asking me, *You ever dropped acid in your eye?* I said *Yes* like an experienced acid dropper, no clue what they were talking about, but knowing Yes sounded better than No. They laughed, I laughed, we all knew I was lying. They wanted me to get in the vehicle. I mumbled some excuse why not. The real reason was I Knew I would have somehow died and even though I wanted to die, I wanted to choose when/where/how. They drove off.

Next thing ya know, the ginger was a dead Dead Head. It was a classic country kid four-wheeling accident. It took out the boy-man too. My friend and I were suddenly widows. Our futures looked dark and boring. I begged Mom to let me go to the wake. She didn't understand my interest, my connection.

To this day, I have both their prayer cards in my possession.

PHONE CALL - SUMMER AFTERNOON

KASSIE

I can tell there's more here.

MEG

It needs work. I just…(hesitates)

How do I tell a story I've never told out loud or even to myself? I mean, I'm not sure I can go there. I worry people won't believe me or that I'll get sued. Like, am I making all this up now just because I'm writing a book and I need material?

KASSIE

No. You know what you experienced.

MEG

It's just too insane to put into words. I was truly out of my mind at that time. This was in that space between the first time I tried to turn him in and the second time. So we both knew what was going on, I even had a name for it now and I knew I had some leverage or power. I was rubbing it in his face, making him worry I was going to squeal. Maybe I was trying to get him to kill me or something?

(thinking pause)

I was drinking any alcohol I could get my hands on and parading around the pool in this tube top Tommy Hilfiger bikini. I would linger around the swim-up bar trying to pick up who I thought were businessmen but they were probably just dads on vacation. I guess I was into dads? I was telling them I was eighteen, nineteen, twenty-one. I was twelve! But of course if these guys had been caught they woulda said, "BUT she said she was eighteen!" There was no way I looked eighteen.

I met this local guy in the pool one day and just kissed him. He didn't even ask for it. We met later that night on some lounge chairs and I didn't speak Spanish so we couldn't even talk. I have no idea how we even arranged to meet up.(laughs)

I let him ravage me and it was one of the only times I could breathe on that trip. Then he took some kinda nude photos of me. I wonder where those are!(sigh)

It was summer and I was in Aruba! I'm still in awe of my privilege, but it was a privileged Hell!(laughs)

By the time I got home I was so sick. So sick and so tan. I remember my mom saying something like, "I barely recognize you." It felt like what you'd say to some returning soldier. My glands were swollen out of the side of my neck and I had no energy, no spark. Turns out I had fucking mono! The kissing disease! (loud laughter)

Marilyn was the third person that year whom I'd suspected of having an incest history and who was then diagnosed with an autoimmune disease–a disease in which the body starts attacking itself.
–Bessel van der Kolk, MD

KASSIE

Oh my god...

(gets cut off)

MEG

Recently I looked up the definition of mono and it said prolonged lassitude. I didn't know what lassitude meant so I looked that up and it said a state of physical or mental weariness. Too good! I was so deeply weary of the game I was playing. But I thought I was in control, that it was my choice to play this game. I thought I invented the game! I can't believe my spleen didn't explode!

Without a helping witness, a mistreated child does not regard the damage done to its integrity as a psychic mutilation. It believes that its father truly wanted something positive.
–Alice Miller

KASSIE

You were surviving...

(gets cut off)

MEG

Oh god, then Princess Diana died! It was such a big deal in my house because she was like the divorcee's patron saint. Her funeral was after I got back from Aruba. I know that because it was on the same day as my brother's first college football game. (deep breath in)

So I'm real sick and my mom had to go… I don't blame her… but it was bad timing. I had a sickbed on the floor in front of the TV in our living room and I got up London time to watch the procession and I remember sobbing when her brother spoke, screaming on the inside, just wishing my brothers would protect me or give some stern public speech on my behalf. (sigh)

It's a lot to sort out and carry around. I can feel it stored like toxic waste in my hip creases.

(silence)

KASSIE

I wish we had been recording what you just said because you were perfectly clear.

MEG

It's so much easier to just blurt it out to you than try to write it down and think about style or other people reading it.

(pause)

I guess I need to keep in mind that

it might be helpful for people to hear these things? I remember watching Leaving Neverland and feeling so calm and seen when the guys were saying, "Then Michael asked me to show him my butthole." I wanted to scream, "That's me! I'm on TV!" Hearing those explicit details make me feel like less of a freak. I don't think I can be that explicit though. I have truly juicy details and the urge is to use them but I don't wanna have to prove the legit horror of my abuse. I just want people to know that traumatized folks do things that don't make sense from the outside, ya know? That it's so easy to get addicted and endlessly perpetrate your own stress and pain. That it's a perfectly normal reaction for a young girl who has been raped by her father to then go out and try to fuck "businessmen." (laughs)

KASSIE

UUUUGGGHH! I really wish we had a transcript of this! Maybe you could try rewriting our conversation in script form?

MEG

(weary) I could try… It's kind of like what I did with that telephone play.

KASSIE

Yes, exactly! It might give you a buffer…

(pause)

I'm sorry this happened to you.

MEG

Yeah…

KASSIE

Remember, it's your story to tell.

You get older but your coping stays the same age. And follows you to Europe.

I get drunk to the point of gambling. *Pick a guy, any guy in this bar, and I'll get them to go home with me. If I win, you have to buy me dinner wherever I wanna go and I wanna go somewhere fancy!* They (men I considered my friends) chose a boy with big eyes and soft curls. He stood no chance. I had real skin in the game, my whole hide, so it was a lock bet. He fell directly into the center of my sticky web.

After unprotected sex (no condom, no pill, no plan) in my hotel room, he told me his mom was dead. Then he cried. I was so uncomfortable, so annoyed with the weight of his tears, that I got up and took a bath, leaving him there to suffer alone.

When we departed the next morning, I let him know, *You will never see me again* (I stopped before adding: *like your mother*). It was necessary to hurt him. His pain over the death of his mom had encroached on My Coping. He was keeping food from my starving mouth. The streetcar doors closed forever on his delicate, startled face. I spent the ride staring at the always hungry predator in my reflection, trying to convince myself I was only acting this way because I was in Europe, so far from home.

...people who have suffered in the past, or find themselves implicated in situations in which they are afraid to be accountable, fear that within their group acknowledging some responsibility will mean being denied their need to be heard or cared for.
–Sarah Schulman

Sometimes the yoke you construct to cope is so magnificent you are grateful to be burdened.

I fall asleep. I enter a dream, a nightmare. A shadow is lurking about, ready to pounce. Stress is chugging through my veins. It's this all too familiar feeling that is my trigger.

This is a dream. This stress is not real. I am safer than when I'm awake.

I go lucid. I get myself to The Field as quickly as possible. This often consists of opening a door, a window, lifting a rug to reveal a staircase. The Field is rolling hills of green uniform grass cut to precision by the teeth of cows—I never see the cows but Know they are the mowers. The sky is movie blue. There is a road and telephone poles in the distance but I can make them disappear. I stand on top of any hill. I look down at the ground to find I am tens of feet tall, then I am inches short. I reach down and take the position of a runner at the start of a race. Hands grab the ground in front of me, pulling. The grass wrinkles up as a cashmere sweater does. With one swift yank, I use the handfuls to catapult myself off the ground into the sky like a fuel-less plane, a glider, I guess you'd say. I float fast. I release all stress, free of self, free of family, free of pain. I gently land. I blast off again and again and again. When I wake up, I never know where I am.

4 hours and 41 minutes remaining, calculates the screen on the back of the seat in front of me. I try to turn the screen off but Air Canada turns it back on without my consent. I turn it off again. It turns on again, *For your convenience.* The categories on the home screen are shapeshifting every few moments to ensure multiple impressions.

Entertainment / Food & Shopping / Aeroplan Flight
Map / Tag Heur™ Boutique Now Open
Games / About This 787
Stay Connected / Arrival Info

By straining through the cracks between the seats and leaning into the aisle, I can spy on many other screens. Not just seat screens but phone screens, laptop screens, tablet screens, watch screens; tapping, swiping, typing, clicking, scrolling, searching, purchasing. How can it be that we can shop this many tens of thousands of feet up in the air? Shop till you drop...out of the sky (I should admit, I bought a moisturizer at the airport (while I'm at it, I went for a manicure on the day of the big climate march)). I always avert my eyes as the flight attendants charade the aisle, hawking Swarovski crystals and Lindt chocolate (do they get a commission?).

If I buy a useless toy or breakfast food or face cream that is available on the market and has been advertised, I am giving extra value, not only to the producers and sellers of the product, but also to the market process, without which I would not have bought it. Advertising elicits the free gift of our attention endlessly... The central recipient of our attention for most of our lives is the market and all the varieties of our participation in it.
–Genevieve Vaughan

Is shopping our most destructive form of coping?

If we could cope in communion with nature,
there would be no use for the economy.

A pungent blob of uterus lining slides down the bowl of the toilet into a new hole. I’m not pregnant in the pandemic. I pray for anyone who needs an abortion during this time.

Abortion #1

I was a student on family insurance and thought if I got the cheapest option, no one would notice it on whatever kind of paperwork insurance produces and sends to the attention of parents. No one warned how loud and painful it would be, the sound of Bearing Down mixed with the sucking of the vacuum. I passed out to survive. I woke up in a narrow warm low-lit room lined with women in medical La-Z-Boys. It felt like only our reactions separated us. Some were silent and dozing, one woman was doing paperwork as if she had to leave and argue a case, one woman was crying quietly, and I was desperately holding back puke.

The guy who supplied the semen came by later that evening with an offering of weed. Eva hovered over me protectively. I felt insulted but You Know I Smoked That Weed.

Abortion #2

No more family insurance. I couldn't afford to be knocked out, but I couldn't manage it awake again. It cost $400 to be put into a twilight sleep. This procedure occurred in a particular state where you had to come in first to confirm pregnancy, go home and *think about it* for x amount of days, and then schedule the procedure, which depended on their schedule, not yours. I remember walking out of the clinic thinking most women must not come back and not because they thought about it and changed their minds but due to a lack of time. What if you wanted an abortion at eighteen weeks and they couldn't fit you in until three weeks from then? You'd be over the legal time limit and you wouldn't be able to get it, right?*

I used this abortion to quit the steak house hostess job. Kelly called and quit for me. *She won't be back to work. She had to have an abortion. I'll come pick up her last check.* The things friends do for each other. I'll never forget her running back to the car, grinning with the check, like we had pulled off some sort of heist. We gladly forgot I had already worked for that money.

*Delay can be a tactical tool of control. I have noticed that misogynists are often late. They make you wait so that your confidence and certainty evaporate. They arrive and seamlessly grab the reins you didn't even realize you dropped.

Abortion #3

The morning was cold enough to see breath. Boyfriend at the time and I had to walk through a pro-life picket line to get in. I was high on relief, knowing when I walked out post-procedure that I would no longer forever be connected to this man.

For some unknown reason I craved and I ate Taco Bell after all three abortions. I regret only the Taco Bell.

Shame, to me, is hiding information that reveals common human experiences, contradictions and mistakes.
–Sarah Schulman

It wasn't realistic for me to use abortion-as-birth-control forever but The Pill, off and on it from fifteen to twenty-five, made me wanna die. I swore it off forever when day two of a dishwashing job in a new town found me contemplating suicide with every big knife I scrubbed. I sheepishly asked one of the waitresses (that I had literally just met at the start of the shift), *Has The Pill ever made you feel...crazy?* She looked at me as if I was on a ledge and told me to *get off That Pill right away.* She had almost killed herself because of That Pill.

I Knew there had to be another way to keep from getting pregnant.

I decided to place trust in the unlicensed women in my life.
–Megan Magray

*One way is to track the white stuff in your underwear and it's free!** Molly lays it out for me. She is realistic about the risks but adamant about the benefits. I'm certain that I will get it all wrong and be back at Taco Bell in no time. *No, there's no wrong way to be alive.*

Without the women in my life, both living and dead, I would have been roadkill simply ages ago. All women benefit from concentrating our energy on the power within our own circle of friends, creating informal health collectives where we discuss things like our bodies and our selves.
–Inga Muscio

*Fertility Awareness Methods–or FAMs or Fate's Answering Machine–can be used to avoid or attain pregnancy, track and prepare for moods and menstruation, monitor overall health or as a tool to accumulate self-knowledge. *And it's free!*

It's no fun to be sixteen at the county STD clinic. It gets worse when the nurse is a family friend. Mrs. McClintock. I have known her since I was in first grade. I was close with her youngest daughter for many years but we drifted apart upon entering high school. It's been a while since I've seen Mrs. McClintock.

Don't tell my mom.

Meg, legally I can't say a word. You did the right thing coming here. I'm proud of you. Let's begin with you telling me exactly why you are here...

She doesn't bat an eye. She's seen it all. My shame wanes. I'm just a person living a life.

It's okay, honey. In the future, just try to avoid going from vagina to anus and back again.

Everything
is
Temporary

July 5, 2020. Birthday. I'm still here. One person living one life. Mistakes abound, shame rarely at arm's length. Mom pines, *You are now older than I was when I gave birth to you. Time is galloping.* I'm impressed by her use of the word *galloping* but I don't really fear time as some horse I'll never be able to keep up with. I don't want to domesticate any animal. I simply dislike the yearly reminder of compound trauma. Being born on the hangover of America's Independence Day is to be born hyper-haunted.

Fellow-citizens; above your national, tumultuous joy, I hear the mournful wail of millions! whose chains, heavy and grievous yesterday, are, to-day, rendered more intolerable by the jubilee shouts that reach them.
–Frederick Douglass

I see your pain and wish I could banish it to the forest but I know that is not how trauma works and might we too be banishing the art? Heaven forbid. Jennifer often knows what to say when I'm off-centered. I hold the opposites in my hands and momentarily accept their equal weight. I feel myself level off:
This will always hurt.
This is temporary.

Soon enough me and the United States of America will be dust.

EXT./INT. FRONT STOOP/FOYER

Loud knock on front door. Meg runs downstairs to open it. Two men in business attire with binders greet her.

MAN 1

Do you remember us? We met last summer?

MEG

Uhhh...(remembering) yeah, yeah I re-member.

MAN 2

We came back to ask if you've heard what the Bible says…

(gets cut off)

MAN 1

We want to know, are you worried about the future?

MEG

Nope.

MAN 2

(unbelieving tone)

No?

MEG

(forceful)

No.

MAN 1
(poking)
Not even a little bit?

MEG
Listen, I've been to hell and I'm not afraid to die.

I WENT
TO
HeLL
AND ALL I GOT WAS
THIS T-SHIRT

WORKS CITED

"American English Beatles Tribute Band." americanenglish.com. Accessed May 9, 2020.

Artaud, Antonin. *Selected Writings*, edited by Susan Sontag, translated by Helen Weaver. Farrar, Straus, and Giroux, 1976.

"Big Johnson." *Wikipedia*, Wikimedia Foundation, September 24, 2020, en.wikipedia.org/wiki/Big_Johnson.

Borger, Julian. "A Glance, a Nod, Silence and Death." *Guardian*, June 11, 2001.

Boxer, Sarah. "The Banality of Terror: Dreams of Holy War Over a Quiet Evening." *New York Times*, December 16, 2001.

Clinton, Bill. "Clinton's Grand Jury Testimony, Part 4." *Washington Post*, September 21, 1998.

Cooper, Kelly-Leigh. "Oklahoma City Bombing: The Day Domestic Terror Shook America." *BBC News*, April 18, 2020.

Douglass, Frederick. "What to the Slave Is the Fourth of July?" Rochester Ladies' Anti-Slavery Society Independence Day Event, July 5, 1852, Corinthian Hall, Rochester, NY. Keynote address.

Frame, Janet. *To the Is-Land*. George Braziller, 1982.

Frankl, Viktor. *Man's Search for Meaning*. 1959. Beacon Press, 2006.

Greacen, Chris. "CO_2 Emissions from an EA-18G Growler." *Citizens of Ebey's Reserve*, January 1, 2015.

Hamilton, Edith. *Mythology: Timeless Tales of Gods and Heroes*. Little, Brown and Company, 1942.

Kolk, Bessel van der. *The Body Keeps the Score: Brain, Mind, and Body in the Healing of Trauma*. Viking, 2014.

"List of Major League Players Suspended for Domestic Violence." *Wikipedia*, Wikimedia Foundation, September 13, 2020, en.wikipedia.org/wiki/List_of_Major_League_Baseball_players_suspended_for_domestic_violence.

Luckiesh, M. *Visual Illusions: Their Causes, Characteristics and Applications.* D. Van Nostrand Company, 1922.

Luling, Todd Van. "11 Things You Probably Didn't Know about the Beatles, Even If You're a Superfan." *Huffington Post*, August 5, 2014.

Magray, Megan. "The Left Case for Fertility Awareness." *Nation*, December 26, 2019.

Maracle, Lee. *My Conversations with Canadians.* Book*hug, 2017.

Miller, Alice. *Breaking Down the Wall of Silence: The Liberating Experience of Facing Painful Truth.* Dutton, 1991.

Muscio, Inga. *Cunt: A Declaration of Independence.* Seal Press, 1998.

Ring, Sheryl. "Towards a New Approach to MLB's Domestic Violence Policy." *Beyond the Box Score*, October 23, 2019.

Schulman, Sarah. *Conflict Is Not Abuse: Overstating Harm, Community Responsibility, and the Duty of Repair.* Arsenal Pulp Press, 2017.

U.S. Girls. "Telephone Play No. 1." *Half Free*, 4AD, 2015. Vinyl LP.

Vaughan, Genevieve. *For-Giving: A Feminist Criticism of Exchange.* Plain View Press, 1997.

Westover, Tara. *Educated: A Memoir.* Random House, 2018.

Zerubavel, Eviatar. *The Elephant in the Room: Silence and Denial in Everyday Life.* Oxford University Press, 2006.

Ziezulewicz, Geoff. "The Navy's Probe into Sky Penis." *Navy Times*, May 13, 2019.

READING THAT LED ME TO WRITE THIS BOOK

Adnan, Etel. *Surge.* Nightboat Books, 2018.

____. *The Sun on the Tongue*, edited by Bonnie Marranca and Klaudia Ruschkowski. PAJ Publications, 2018.

Baker, Nicholson. *Human Smoke: The Beginnings of World War II, the End of Civilization*. Simon & Schuster, 2008.

Baudrillard, Jean. "Radical Thought." In *The Conspiracy of Art*, edited by Sylvère Lotringer, translated by Ames Hodges. Semiotext(e), 2005.

Chute, Carolyn. *The Beans of Egypt, Maine*. Ticknor & Fields, 1985.

Cixous, Hélène. *The Hélène Cixous Reader*, edited by Susan Sellers. Routledge, 1994.

Deraniyagala, Sonali. *Wave*. Alfred A. Knopf, 2013.

Dumont, Marilyn. *A Really Good Brown Girl*. Brick Books, 1996.

Ensler, Eve. *The Apology*. Bloomsbury Publishing, 2019.

Estés, Clarissa Pinkola. *Women Who Run with the Wolves: Myths and Stories of the Wild Woman Archetype*. Random House, 1992.

Hofstadter, Dan. *The Earth Moves: Galileo and the Roman Inquisition*. W. W. Norton & Company, 2009.

Ice Cream. "Dove's Cry." *Fed Up*, 2019. Vinyl LP.

Olsen, Tillie. *Silences*. Delacorte Press/Seymour Lawrence, 1978.

Pendleton, Adam. *Black Dada Reader*, edited by Stephen Squibb. Koenig Books, 2017.

Redvers, Tunchai. *Fireweed*. Kegedonce Press, 2019.

Vaughan, Genevieve, editor. *Women and the Gift Economy: A Radically Different Worldview Is Possible*. Inanna Publications and Education Inc., 2007.

Washington, RA. *Body*. GTK Press, 2016.

Telephone Play No. 1

(telephone ringing, telephone answered)

WOMAN 1

Hello?

WOMAN 2

Hey. How you doing, babe?

WOMAN 1

I'm okay. I'm just still in bed. Bad dream.

WOMAN 2

Your dreams are always bad.

WOMAN 1

I know. It's nothing new. It's just…

WOMAN 2

What happened this time?

WOMAN 1

Ummm…my dad sent me a digital file folder and in it were all these nude photos of me as a child.

WOMAN 2

(knowing laugh) Sounds realistic.

WOMAN 1
I know. The thing is I was kind of hot stuff. I mean, I don't know, I looked good, so it was sort of confusing.

WOMAN 2
Oh—oh god. Fathers and daughters.

WOMAN 1
Yeah, yeah… What about mothers and sons?

WOMAN 2
Yeah, but fathers and daughters.

WOMAN 1
Yeah, but mothers and daughters, man, fuck.

WOMAN 2
Yeah, but there's just kind of no comparison.(laughs)

WOMAN 1
The worst is fathers and sons.

WOMAN 2
Oh god, yeah. Okay, that's the worst.

WOMAN 1
At least I'm no one's son.

WOMAN 2
Thank god for that! You'd definitely be

one of those sons that turns into a fascist dictator.

WOMAN 1

Yeah. Instead I'm just another woman with no self-esteem.

(studio audience laugh track)

ACKNOWLEDGEMENTS

Kassie Richardson, the unflappable editor/doula of this manuscript.

Logan T. Sibrel, the only person I could trust to illustrate the text earnestly and with humor.

Dee Dee Dunklau, the woman who gave birth to me and my of love reading.

Maximilian Turnbull, the man I love to debate and learn with.

LuLu Hazel Turnbull, "Woman 2" of Telephone Play No. 1.

The Toronto Public Library and the Cambridge Public Library, the suppliers of work space, research materials, and photocopiers.

Flaming Fingers Word Processing, who did the typing I couldn't face.

Malcolm Sutton, Hazel & Jay MillAr at Book*hug, the providers/navigators of the opportunity to write this text.

PHOTO: EMMA MC INTYRE

MEG REMY is a multidisciplinary artist and performer. Originally from Illinois, she is established as one of the most acclaimed songwriters and performers to emerge from the eclectic underground music scene in Toronto where she currently lives. Primarily known as the creative force behind the musical entity U.S. Girls, her celebrated discography spans early experimental works released on the Siltbreeze label, and includes three Polaris Prize shortlisted albums released by 4AD: *Half Free* (2015), *In a Poem Unlimited* (2018), and *Heavy Light* (2020). Both *Half Free* and *In a Poem Unlimited* also garnered Juno nominations for best Alternative album. Meg has toured extensively through Europe and North America, establishing a reputation for politically astute commentary and theatrical performances with her extended U.S. Girls band, named the best live act of 2018 by *Paste Magazine*. During this time Remy has maintained a visual arts practice, exhibiting collage work and directing several music videos and other video artworks including her short film *Woman's Advocate* (2014), in which she also performed. *Begin by Telling* is her first book.

COLOPHON

Manufactured as the first edition of
Begin by Telling in the spring of 2021 by
Book*hug Press

Edited for the press by Kassie Richardson
and Malcolm Sutton
Copy edited by Stuart Ross
Illustrations by Logan T. Sibrel
Cover by Meg Remy
Type by Malcolm Sutton

bookhugpress.ca